CW01432575

Original title:
The Spirit of the Fir

Author: Linda Leevike
ISBN HARDBACK: 978-9908-1-1789-8
ISBN PAPERBACK: 978-9908-1-1790-4
ISBN EBOOK: 978-9908-1-1791-1

Enchantment in Every Needle

Beneath the boughs, a laughter grows,
Twinkling lights in soft repose.
Children's smiles, the joy we chase,
Nature's beauty, a warm embrace.

Snowflakes fall, a shimmering veil,
Whispers of winds tell a tale.
Every needle, a spark of cheer,
Holidays bright with those we hold dear.

A Path Through the Pines

In the woods where shadows play,
Pine-scented air leads the way.
Step by step, a journey bright,
Among the trees, hearts take flight.

Laughter echoes, a gentle tune,
Starlit skies bring nights of June.
Each path winding, a dance of glee,
Nature's magic, wild and free.

Heartstrings of the Forest

Echoes of joy in the air abound,
Nature's heartbeat is a joyous sound.
Every rustle, each joyful cheer,
Brings together everyone near.

Leaves twirl down in a vibrant show,
Whispers of secrets through branches flow.
With every step, our spirits align,
In the forest's embrace, all is divine.

The Dance of the Evergreens

Evergreens sway to the music bright,
Underneath the moon's soft light.
A festive air fills every space,
With twinkling stars, a warm embrace.

Children twirling in pure delight,
Laughter ringing through the night.
Each moment shared, a treasure bestowed,
In the forest's heart, love is sowed.

Whispers of Evergreen

In the warm glow of twinkling lights,
Joy dances on a crisp evening breeze.
Laughter and melodies fill the nights,
Fingers entwined beneath the trees.

Ornaments shimmer, tales unfold,
Families gather, hearts interlace.
The magic of stories, dreams retold,
As moments are painted with love's embrace.

Echoes of cheer in every sound,
Songs of the season, sweetly sung.
Together we stand on this joyful ground,
With spirits of winter forever young.

Heartbeat of the Conifer

Beneath the stars, lanterns sway,
The forest hums with joy tonight.
Nature's heartbeat guides our play,
As we bask in the sparkling light.

Soft whispers weave through the pines,
A celebration of life in bloom.
With every laugh, the spirit shines,
Chasing away the winter's gloom.

Friends and family gather round,
Sharing stories, dreams, and cheer.
In this grove, love knows no bound,
Creating memories we hold dear.

Echoes in the Canopy

Treetops sway as night unfolds,
The branches catch the laughter's flight.
Echoes of joy, timeless tales told,
Underneath a blanket of starlight.

Glimmers of hope in every leaf,
Dancing shadows play on the ground.
In this haven, we find relief,
A symphony of love unbound.

With every heartbeat, the forest sings,
Notes of happiness whisper through.
Together we share what the season brings,
In the warmth of friendship, ever true.

Secrets of the Timber

In the heart of the wood, secrets gleam,
Fires crackle with warmth and delight.
Under the moon, we draw the dream,
Sharing our hopes in the soft twilight.

Golden sparks fly into the night,
Each flicker a wish danced to the sky.
In this moment, everything feels right,
As laughter weaves through the branches high.

Twinkling lights on the forest floor,
Boundless joy in the crisp, cool air.
Together we cherish forevermore,
In the embrace of love, free from care.

Resilience in the Roots

In the heart of the soil, life does bloom,
With laughter and joy, we chase away gloom.
Tiny seeds unfurl, reaching for the sun,
A dance of persistence, together we run.

Through storms and shadows, we stand ever strong,
Roots intertwining, where all of us belong.
Celebrating each win, every step that we take,
Bound by connection, together we make.

Song of the Forest

Whispers of leaves, a melodious grace,
Birds chirping joyfully, each finds its place.
Under the canopy, sunlight cascades,
Nature's sweet symphony, never ever fades.

Colors so vibrant, a festival of hue,
Dancing in harmony, me and you.
Each branch sways gently, a rhythm divine,
In the heart of the forest, we happily dine.

Guardians of the Green

In fields of emerald, we gather with cheer,
Rustling of branches, the moment is near.
Hands joined together, we nurture and tend,
For nature's own bounty, we celebrate, friend.

Around roaring fires, stories unfold,
Of legends and dreams, in warmth we behold.
With every green shoot, a promise anew,
Guardians of the green, in all that we do.

Shadows in the Grove

Under the twilight, where soft breezes play,
Gathering shadows, the colors decay.
Yet in this dim light, laughter remains,
Binding us closer, despite gentle rains.

With lanterns aglow, our spirits take flight,
Creating new memories, chasing the night.
In shadows we roam, hand in hand we glow,
A festivity sparkles, in the heart of the grove.

Soul of the Needle

In the forest's heart, we gather bright,
Whispers of joy in the soft moonlight.
Golden threads weave tales untold,
Where laughter and warmth break the cold.

With every stitch, the fabric sings,
Dancing like stars on the hands of kings.
Embrace the gift that the needle gives,
Where the soul of the needle forever lives.

Guardians of the Glade

Beneath the boughs, the sentries stand,
Nature's friends, a gentle band.
Harmonies played on a silver flute,
Echo in every leaf and root.

With twinkling eyes, they watch with glee,
Guardians bright of the jubilee.
In every rustle, they sing along,
Creating a tapestry, cheerful and strong.

Embrace of the Pine

In the whispering pines, a charm unfolds,
A sanctuary where laughter holds.
Branches sway in a festive dance,
Inviting the souls to take a chance.

Candles aglow in the twilight air,
Hearts entwined in the magic rare.
Nature's embrace, warm and divine,
Celebrating life with every pine.

Dreams Beneath the Boughs

Beneath the boughs where dreams take flight,
Imagination sings in the starry night.
Festooned with wishes, the air so bright,
Joy sparkles softly, a wondrous sight.

Gathered together, we share our glow,
Tales of adventure in whispers flow.
In this enchanted, serene retreat,
The dance of dreams is a merry treat.

Tranquility in Trunks

Beneath the boughs, the silence hums,
Whispers of peace where the heart succumbs.
Warm sunlight dapples a soft green floor,
Nature's embrace, forevermore.

Laughter dances on the gentle breeze,
As children play among the trees.
Joy echoes through the shifting leaves,
In tranquil spots where the spirit believes.

Fir's Whispered Dreams

In the forest draped in shades of gold,
Fir trees stand tall with stories untold.
Dreams weave through branches, flicker and soar,
Whispers of magic, we long to explore.

Glimmers of starlight guide us each night,
Fireside gatherings, hearts feeling light.
Songs of the earth fill the air with glee,
Our souls are stitched into this tapestry.

Enchanted by the Evergreen

Evergreen giants in the moonlit glow,
A festival spirit, inviting us slow.
With twinkling lights, we gather near,
Cherishing moments, the ones we hold dear.

Lively conversations echo through the air,
Filling the night with laughter and care.
Each friendly face brings warmth to our hearts,
In this enchanted world, where wonder imparts.

Emblems of Resilience

Through the seasons, the trees stand tall,
Emblems of strength, they weather it all.
Roots deep in earth, don't shy from the storm,
In every challenge, they find a new form.

Celebrate life, embrace every turn,
In the warmth of friendship, our spirits burn.
Together we sing, our voices unite,
In the heart of the forest, we find pure delight.

The Language of Trees

Whispers among the leaves do sway,
Dancing light leads the playful day.
Roots intertwine in joyful ground,
Nature's laughter is all around.

Branches reach like hands in cheer,
Their stories told in scents so clear.
Together they twirl in the warm breeze,
A festival of life in the trees.

Sunlight filters, a golden hue,
Painting shadows where dreams come true.
In every rustle, a tune so sweet,
A symphony where earth and sky meet.

Celebrate with every sigh,
Underneath this vast, blue sky.
With every color, spirit flies,
In the language of trees, joy never dies.

Twilight in the Thicket

As day gives way to soft twilight,
The thicket glows in fading light.
Crickets sing their evening song,
While shadows stretch ever long.

Fireflies blink like tiny stars,
Guiding pathways, near and far.
In whispered secrets, breezes play,
A dance unfolds at end of day.

Leaves shimmer under a moonlit glance,
Inviting all to join the dance.
The air is thick with scents divine,
Beneath the trees, our hearts entwine.

In thickets deep, we find our peace,
As nature hums, our worries cease.
With laughter shared among friends,
Twilight's magic never ends.

Nature's Resilient Heart

From seeds of hope, great forests rise,
A testament under the skies.
Through storms and sun, they stand so tall,
Nature's heart, it beats for all.

Blooming flowers in vibrant array,
Wrap the earth in a bright bouquet.
Each petal tells a tale of grace,
In the tapestry of this place.

Rivers laugh in joyous streams,
Reflecting all our sunlit dreams.
Mountains sing in echoes strong,
In harmony where souls belong.

Through every season, ebbs and flows,
Nature's spirit, forever grows.
In every leaf a story starts,
Whispering tales of resilient hearts.

The Silence of Ancient Woods

In ancient woods where time stands still,
A silence lingers, soft and chill.
Moss carpets the paths we tread,
Whispers of nature in echoes spread.

Gnarled branches hold the tales untold,
Secrets kept in the arms of old.
Each step echoes, profound and deep,
Inviting you into thoughts to keep.

Sunbeams filter through the leaves,
Painting stories that nature weaves.
In their stillness, a wisdom shared,
An ancient world, lovingly bared.

Embrace the quiet, breathe it in,
Let nature's calm wash over sin.
In the silence, much is found,
The heart of woods, a sacred ground.

Whispering Pines

In the glade where laughter sings,
Pines sway gently, their secrets cling.
Beneath the sky, so bright and clear,
Joyful moments, friends draw near.

Candles flicker, dancing light,
Songs of joy fill the night.
Wondrous tales spun in the air,
Grateful hearts, love to share.

Solace in the Shadow

Beneath the bows, we find our peace,
Nature's whispers never cease.
Laughter echoes through the trees,
In the shade, the world's at ease.

Picnics laid on emerald grass,
Moments cherished, seasons pass.
Fireflies twinkle, stars aglow,
In silence, friendships grow.

Life Among the Needles

Amid the needles, life unfolds,
A story rich, forever told.
Rustling leaves, a gentle breeze,
Harmony in nature's keys.

Gatherings under endless skies,
Where laughter mingles with soft sighs.
Songs of the forest, sweet and bright,
Celebrate the warmth of night.

Breath of the Forest

Awash with scents of pine and earth,
Each moment sings of nature's birth.
Children's laughter, spirits high,
Underneath the canvas sky.

Drifting petals, colors bold,
Stories of the forest told.
Together under twilight's gleam,
We weave a shared, enchanting dream.

Forest's Gentle Breaths

In the forest where laughter sings,
Leaves whisper secrets on soft wings.
Colors dance in the eager sun,
Nature's joy has just begun.

Breezes twirl, a festive cheer,
Echoes of the wild draw near.
Every creature joins the play,
Celebrating a vibrant day.

Breath of the Mountains

Mountains rise with grandeur bright,
Wrapped in snow, a pure delight.
Clouds drift by, a festive parade,
Shadows play in the sun's cascade.

Rivers sing with sparkling glee,
Whispers of nature, wild and free.
Under twilight's shimmering glow,
Hearts unite in joy below.

Guardians of the Green

Tall trees stand in festive rows,
Guardians where the wild wind blows.
Beneath their shade, children laugh,
Life's simple joys, a joyful path.

Flowers bloom in vibrant hues,
Painted skies with radiant views.
Nature's record, old yet new,
A symphony of life in view.

A Tapestry of Trunks

In a tapestry where shadows play,
Trunks together weave the day.
Sunlight drips like golden rain,
Natures pulse, a soothing vein.

With each step, the earth does hum,
In this place, our hearts become.
Festive spirits fill the air,
In the forest's gentle care.

Shadows of the Old Growth

Beneath the ancient trees we dance,
With laughter woven in each glance.
The whispers of the leaves above,
Embrace our spirits, spread the love.

Sunbeams trickle through the boughs,
A golden touch, and there it bows.
In shadows deep, we find our way,
To celebrate this festive day.

Mossy carpets, soft and bright,
Guide our steps into the light.
With every heartbeat, joy expands,
Together here, we make our plans.

The old growth speaks in rustling tones,
Of memories shared; we're never alone.
So gather 'round, let spirits sway,
In shadows rich, we'll find our play.

Twilight Under the Green

As twilight falls, the stars ignite,
A tapestry of dreams in sight.
The boughs embrace the evening's glow,
Beneath the green, our laughter flows.

Fireflies twinkle, like joy in flight,
They weave through branches, pure delight.
With every flicker, stories spun,
In whispers shared, we become one.

The air is thick with festive cheer,
As shadows dance, bringing us near.
In unity, we find our grace,
Under the green, a sacred space.

Drink deep the night, let hearts rejoice,
In this moment, we find our voice.
Together we revel in nature's tight weave,
In twilight's arms, we shall believe.

A Glimpse of Verdant Wisdom

Through emerald leaves, the wisdom flows,
In silent murmurs, nature knows.
The roots entwined, a story told,
Of seasons passed and dreams of old.

Beneath the canopy, we unite,
In laughter, love, a pure delight.
With dragonflies as guests of honor,
They flutter here, our joy grows fonder.

Each bloom a burst of rich embrace,
Inviting us to find our place.
With each heartbeat, a festive tune,
The verdant wisdom calls us soon.

So come, let's dance on nature's stage,
In this moment, free and sage.
With every breath, let spirits soar,
A glimpse of wisdom, we adore.

The Light Between the Trees

In the hush of woods, a laughter streams,
A glimmering light, a dance of dreams.
The trees stand tall, weaving their spell,
In realms of wonder, where stories dwell.

Sunbeams filter through leafy veils,
A spectacle bright, where joy exhales.
We gather close, our hearts aligned,
The light between the trees defined.

Echoes of buoyant voices rise,
Carried high beneath the skies.
With every step and twirl we take,
We paint the air, our world awake.

So let us roam through nature's grace,
Together in this sacred place.
For in the light, we find our glee,
In harmony with all that we see.

Shadows in the Forest

In the glade where laughter sings,
Sunlight dances, joy it brings.
Whispers of the leaves above,
Nature's symphony of love.

Around the trunks, the children play,
Bright blossoms dance, a grand ballet.
Footsteps light on mossy ground,
Echoing the joy around.

Bubbles rise in the warm air,
Tales are shared without a care.
With each cheer, the shadows sway,
Festive spirits here will stay.

As the day begins to fade,
Twinkling lights, the night parade.
With every smile, the forest glows,
In this haven, happiness flows.

Symphony of the Spruce

Beneath the boughs of timeless trees,
A chorus sings on gentle breeze.
Strings of laughter, soft and clear,
Weaving joy for all to hear.

With every step, the rhythm grows,
Melodies in the forest flows.
Drumming heartbeats, swift and wild,
Nature's song, forever styled.

Glimmers twinkle, shadows dance,
Every glance, a fleeting chance.
Notes of joy in the evening air,
A festive spirit everywhere.

As stars emerge in twilight's glow,
The symphony begins to flow.
Vibrant hearts entwine as one,
A celebration just begun.

Growth Among the Giants

Standing tall, the giants reign,
Whispering tales of joy and pain.
Among their roots, the flowers bloom,
Creating color, dispelling gloom.

Sunlight filters through the leaves,
A tapestry that nature weaves.
Children gather, stories shared,
In this haven, hope declared.

Every petal, every sigh,
Mirror dreams that reach the sky.
Joyous laughter fills the air,
In this space, free from care.

Amidst the giants, life takes flight,
Colors blend in pure delight.
With each heartbeat, joy extends,
In this grove, where magic blends.

Echoes of the Conifers

In the hush of the evergreen,
Whispers dance, a festive scene.
Echoes call in gentle tones,
Nature's chorus among the stones.

Twilight sparkles, shadows play,
As laughter melds with fading day.
Branches sway, a rhythmic show,
In this moment, spirits glow.

Every sigh holds tales untold,
In the forest, rich and bold.
With each heartbeat, memories bloom,
Celebrating life in the gloom.

As stars twinkle in darkened skies,
Magic sparkles in our eyes.
In the embrace of towering trees,
We find joy, our hearts at ease.

Silent Guardians of the Glen

Amidst the whispering trees, they stand,
Watching over the land so grand.
With laughter that dances on the breeze,
Silent guardians, they bring us peace.

Beneath the stars that twinkle bright,
They gather 'round in gentle light.
With hearts aglow and joy to share,
Their spirits weave through evening air.

On festive nights, the glen awakes,
Where friendship blooms and laughter shakes.
With every song and every cheer,
The guardians keep our memories near.

In harmony, their voices blend,
A celebration that knows no end.
For in this place, where love is found,
The silent guardians stand their ground.

Timeless Roots

In fields where golden sunbeams play,
The roots of joy take shape each day.
Where laughter rings and stories flow,
Timeless roots in hearts do grow.

Beneath the boughs, we gather near,
With every smile, we cast out fear.
In the warmth of friends, our spirits rise,
As tunes of love fill summer skies.

A tapestry of colors bright,
We dance and twirl in pure delight.
These moments shared, forever last,
Timeless roots, binding joy to past.

Through seasons changing, we will stay,
In festive circles, come what may.
These roots will hold us, strong and true,
In every shade, a vibrant hue.

Echoes of the Pine

In the forest deep, where echoes call,
The scent of pine enchants us all.
With laughter soft like morning dew,
Echoes of the pine, ever new.

We gather close, hands intertwined,
In the embrace of nature, so kind.
With every cheer that fills the air,
The echoes of joy linger rare.

Under the branches, shadows dance,
As hearts ignite in merry trance.
The whispers of the pine convey,
A festive mood that guides our way.

With every story shared in glee,
The echoes of love sing wild and free.
In this sacred space, we find our home,
Among the pines, forever roam.

Elders of the Mountain

High above, where the eagles soar,
Elders gather, wisdom in lore.
With tales of old and laughter shared,
Their presence lingers, hearts prepared.

Around the fire, their voices rise,
A symphony beneath the skies.
With every story, the stars ignite,
Elders of the mountain, pure delight.

They sing of seasons, of love and loss,
With every word, we feel the gloss.
In festive moments, their light we seek,
The elders' whispers calm and meek.

Through every trial, they guide the way,
Their laughter rings like bright bouquet.
In the embrace of nature's grace,
Elders of the mountain find their place.

Underneath the Pine's Gaze

Laughter trails through the air, crisp and bright,
Children dance, faces aglow with delight.
Scents of sweet pine mingle with cheer,
Warmth of the season wrapping us near.

Twinkling lights hang like stars in the night,
Songs of the season, hearts taking flight.
Stories shared 'round the crackling fire,
Joy ignites like a spark of desire.

With mugs raised high to the twinkling sky,
Together we bask, no reason to sigh.
Underneath the pine's watchful gaze,
We celebrate life in simple ways.

A tapestry woven of laughter and song,
Memories made where we all belong.
In the shadow of giants, we smile and sway,
Underneath the pine, we cherish the day.

Secrets Wrapped in Bark

Whispers travel on the soft, cool breeze,
Secrets of nature, hidden with ease.
Rustling leaves tell tales of the past,
In their shadows, moments forever cast.

Beneath towering trunks so gnarled and wise,
Lies laughter shared in muffled sighs.
Children's giggles, echoing around,
Life's magic lingers in the ground.

Squirrels play hide-and-seek in the trees,
A festive dance with the buzzing bees.
Underneath the limbs, all worries cease,
In nature's embrace, we find our peace.

With each ring of the tree, a new year turns,
Lessons of life in the quiet we learn.
Wrapped in the bark, secrets entwine,
In this wondrous world, joy will always shine.

Green Sentinels

Green sentinels stand tall and proud,
Guardians of joy in their leafy shroud.
Their branches cradle the sun's golden face,
Creating a haven, a magical space.

Under their watch, the world feels so bright,
Moments of laughter lit by their light.
Together we gather, both young and old,
In whispers of green, our stories unfold.

Picnics laid out on blankets of green,
Feasting on laughter, a joyous scene.
Beneath their shade, time dances slow,
Festive hearts beating with a warm glow.

As dusk drapes gently across the sky,
Fireflies twinkle, a soft serenade sigh.
In the embrace of these giants, we find,
A spirit of festivity intertwined.

The Language of Needles

In the hush of the woods, whispers resound,
The language of needles, a soft spellbound.
Each needle a note in a symphony vast,
A melody woven of memories cast.

Crisp air carries laughter, a sweet, playful tune,
Celebration blooms beneath the bright moon.
Gatherings flourish 'neath branches so wide,
Hearts intertwining, our joy cannot hide.

Glistening dewdrops like gems on the ground,
Nature's embrace, where love can be found.
With every breath, a promise renewed,
In the forest's heart, our spirits imbued.

Around the great trunks, stories unfold,
Festive spirit in whispers of old.
The language of needles, a bright, joyful call,
In the forest's embrace, we welcome it all.

Wisdom in the Wood

In twilight's glow, the branches sway,
Leaves whisper secrets at the close of day.
Old oak stands tall, keeper of tales,
Guiding the hearts where adventure prevails.

Moss carpets paths where shadows dance,
Sunbeams flicker in a magical trance.
Breezes carry laughter, joyful and light,
Nature's own chorus, a festive delight.

Amidst the giants, the spirits rise,
Stars twinkle down from the velvet skies.
With every step, life twirls in cheer,
Embraced by the woods, where all feel near.

Gather 'round logs where stories ignite,
In the circle of friends, the warmth feels right.
Wisdom in whispers, love in the air,
A festive bond spun from nature's rare.

Threads of the Timberland

Golden threads weave through the trees,
A tapestry crafted by whispers and breeze.
Dappled sunlight spills on the ground,
In timberland's heart, joy can be found.

Squirrels chatter, their laughter erupts,
Under the canopy, excitement erupts.
Nature's own fabric, rich and alive,
With every twist, the spirit will thrive.

The pines sway gently, a rhythmic beat,
Echoes of friendship and moments sweet.
Woodland wonders, a chorus of cheer,
In the threads of life, all gatherings near.

So come take part in this joyful weave,
In the woods, believe in what you perceive.
Every heart, every voice, a valued strand,
In the threads of timberland, hand in hand.

Harmony of the Harmony

Beneath the boughs where melodies soar,
Nature's symphony opens each door.
The breeze hums softly, a tranquil tune,
Inviting all hearts, morning till noon.

Crickets and birds join the vibrant play,
Creating a rhythm that brightens the day.
The brook joins in with a bubbling cheer,
A harmony found when loved ones are near.

Sunset paints skies in colors so bold,
Stories of laughter and warmth unfold.
Festivity swells in the air like champagne,
Together we revel, joy we proclaim.

Each note of life dances freely around,
In harmony's embrace, pure joy is found.
Gathered in the beauty, sharing delight,
In the song of the woods, everything feels right.

Emerald Echoes

Emerald leaves with a shimmer so bright,
Dance in the breeze with pure delight.
The forest awakens, each glimmer a smile,
In echoes of joy that stretch for a mile.

Beneath the green canopy, laughter ignites,
Friends come together, chasing the heights.
With every heartbeat, together we sing,
In the emerald whispers, our spirits take wing.

Sunlight cascades like a shower of gold,
Stories and dreams in each moment unfold.
Nature's embrace holds us firmly in place,
In echoes of laughter, we find our grace.

So let's weave our tales in this magical grove,
With emerald echoes, our hearts will rove.
In the lively atmosphere, love we bestow,
In festive embrace, let our joy overflow.

Veil of the Verdant

Beneath the boughs of lively green,
The laughter flows, a joyous scene.
Colors dance in the golden light,
As friends gather, hearts feel bright.

Sweet melodies fill the warm air,
With songs of love, we sing and share.
Each smile a spark, each hug a tune,
In this enchanted afternoon.

Glowing lanterns sway on high,
While fireflies twinkle in the sky.
The scent of blossoms fills our dreams,
Life sparkles as joy redeems.

Together we paint the night so clear,
In this embrace, we cast off fear.
Under the stars, our spirits soar,
In the verdant veil, we are evermore.

Whispers in the Evergreen

In shadows cast by emerald leaves,
The wind hums softly, the heart believes.
Nature's song, a whisper so sweet,
In this moment, our joys complete.

Sunbeams dance on the forest floor,
With every laugh, we long for more.
The pines stand tall, guardians of cheer,
As we gather close, nothing to fear.

The air is rich with playful dreams,
A cascade of joy flows in streams.
With every step on mossy trails,
Adventure calls, the spirit hails.

Under the arch of the evergreens,
We weave our tales, our hearts convene.
Together we soar, hand in hand,
In whispers of joy, together we stand.

Heartwood Dreams

Upon the trunks of ancient trees,
A tapestry woven with whispered breeze.
The sunbeams break through the canopy,
As we share our hopes, wild and free.

Around the fire, stories ignite,
With laughter and love, our spirits take flight.
Each flickering flame a flicker of heart,
In this circle, we'll never part.

With every sip of the sweetest brew,
We toast to dreams that feel so true.
The night unfolds with magic divine,
Together we revel, entwined in time.

In heartwood dreams, our wishes soar,
Crafting moments we can't ignore.
In this warm glow, the world feels right,
Under the stars, our souls ignite.

A Dance Beneath the Canopy

Beneath the branches, we spin and sway,
With joyous hearts, we greet the day.
The rhythm pulses, the music calls,
In a world where adventure enthralls.

With every twirl, the laughter rings,
As nature plays, and the forest sings.
Our feet find flight on the leafy ground,
In this festive embrace, joy is found.

Colors ignite, like flowers in bloom,
As we gather together, hearts consume.
The canopy whispers of dreams and cheer,
In this moment, we draw near.

With dancing shadows and light that beams,
We weave the fabric of wondrous dreams.
In the stillness, under branch and leaf,
Our hearts unite in festive belief.

In the Embrace of Nature

Sunshine dances on our face,
Laughter soars, we find our place.
Flowers bloom in vibrant cheer,
Nature's song, so sweet and clear.

Picnics spread on grassy greens,
Joyful moments, simple scenes.
Children play, their spirits free,
In this land of harmony.

Birds take flight across the skies,
Whispers of the wind arise.
Colors meld in bright array,
In nature's arms, we glide away.

As twilight falls, the stars ignite,
With hearts aglow, we find delight.
In nature's embrace, love thrives,
A festive dance, where joy survives.

Guardians of the Grove

Tall trees stand with steadfast grace,
In their shade, we find our space.
Ancient roots and branches wide,
Whisper secrets, where dreams abide.

Mossy carpets underfoot,
Echoes of the past, so root.
Squirrels chatter, hopping near,
In this grove, we shed our fear.

Sunbeam filters through the leaves,
Nature's magic, the heart believes.
Together we celebrate,
With every step, we elevate.

The tranquil air, a sacred gift,
In harmony, our spirits lift.
Guardians watch with loving eyes,
In this grove, true joy complies.

Breezes Through the Boughs

Gentle breezes, soft and light,
Caress the branches, pure delight.
Dancing leaves, a merry spree,
Whispering secrets just for me.

In the stillness, laughter swells,
Echoing through the forest bells.
Nature's festival, wild and free,
In every breath, serenity.

Sunset paints the sky in gold,
Stories of the day retold.
Stars emerge as night descends,
Where nature's magic never ends.

With every rustle, joy abounds,
In gentle rhythms, love resounds.
Breezes sing their sweet refrain,
In the boughs, we feel no pain.

Leafy Reflections

Mirror lakes reflect the sky,
As leaves flutter, time slips by.
Nature's canvas, hues unfold,
In leafy whispers, tales are told.

Golden rays through branches peek,
Whispers soft, the forest speaks.
A festival of colors bright,
In every glance, pure delight.

We gather here, hand in hand,
In this magical, leafy land.
Joy and laughter fill the air,
In nature's warmth, we plant our care.

The day fades into gentle night,
Stars above ignite the light.
With hearts aglow, we take our flight,
In leafy dreams, we find our might.

Resilient Needles

In the glow of twinkling lights,
Joyful laughter fills the night.
Winter whispers through the air,
Needles dancing everywhere.

Boughs adorned in silver sheen,
Life is vibrant, warm, and green.
Each heart beats with cheerful glee,
Resilient as the evergreen tree.

Children gather, spirits bright,
Songs echo under starry light.
With each cheer, a memory made,
In this festive, joyful parade.

Together we embrace the cheer,
With open hearts, we draw near.
As needles sparkle, spark delight,
In this season, pure and bright.

A Journey Through the Boughs

Wandering through the wooded glade,
Nature's wonders serenade.
Each step brings new sights to share,
In a world beyond compare.

Festive branches arch so wide,
Each leaf a pouch for dreams inside.
Children laugh, their voices soar,
Adventure waits beyond the door.

The scent of pine, a sweet embrace,
In this haven, we find our place.
With every turn, a treasure found,
Joy and wonder all around.

As twilight casts its gentle hue,
The world glimmers in joyful view.
In the heart of nature, we belong,
On this journey, all is song.

Nature's Evergreen Embrace

In fields where the wildflowers bloom,
Nature whispers, dispelling gloom.
Each branch, a story softly weaves,
In emerald whispers, the heart believes.

Gather round the towering trees,
Let the gentle wind bring peace.
With every rustle, life unfolds,
In nature's arms, a tale retold.

Frosty mornings, a frolic bright,
Dancing shadows in the light.
Children play, their laughter free,
In nature's ever-cherished spree.

As we stroll through this lovely place,
Feel the warmth of love's embrace.
With every breath, the joy we trace,
In nature's bond, our hearts find grace.

Tales of the Tallest Trees

Tall and proud, they touch the sky,
Whispers secrets as we pass by.
Each branch holds a festive cheer,
Tales of wonder we long to hear.

Children laugh beneath their shade,
In their stories, memories wade.
Nature's backdrop, vibrant stage,
Turning life's sweet, tender page.

In the twilight's gentle glance,
Leaves sway softly, trees advance.
With every hug and joyful sigh,
The tallest trees, our spirits fly.

Embrace the joy, the life they bring,
In their shadows, hearts take wing.
Together here, we find our grace,
In nature's grand, embracing space.

Life in the Evergreen

In the shade of towering trees,
Laughter dances on the breeze.
Bright ribbons flow and twirl,
Every heart begins to whirl.

Sunlight glimmers on green leaves,
Joyous spirits, everyone believes.
Colors burst in vibrant cheer,
Life's magic is gathered here.

With friends and family near at hand,
We gather close in this lush land.
Songs of life fill up the air,
Unity shines, a treasure rare.

As daylight fades, we light the night,
Stars above twinkle with delight.
In evergreen life, we find our way,
A festive bond, come what may.

Harmony of the Needle and Wood

A symphony of rustling pine,
In the woods where hearts align.
Nature sings in a joyful tune,
Underneath the smiling moon.

Whispers of the trees surround,
In their shade, pure peace is found.
Needles drop, soft and light,
We gather close, our hearts ignite.

The air is filled with scents divine,
Gathered friends and mugs of wine.
Every moment, laughter flows,
In this harmony, love grows.

As dusk descends, we join as one,
Underneath the setting sun.
In the needle's grace, we stay,
Festive warmth guides our way.

Wanderlust Among the Conifers

Footsteps lead through paths unseen,
Where conifers stand, tall and green.
A journey filled with tales to weave,
In their presence, we believe.

Golden sunlight, a welcome glow,
Guides our hearts where breezes blow.
Adventure calls from every side,
In this forest, we abide.

With every corner, new sights appear,
Echoes of laughter, sweet and clear.
Together we explore the scene,
Wanderlust flows in every dream.

As stories bloom, the night unfolds,
In the warmth of joy, we are bold.
Among conifers, we share our song,
In this festive place, we belong.

Stories in the Boughs

Underneath the ancient trees,
Nature whispers on the breeze.
Boughs hold stories, rich and deep,
In their shadow, memories leap.

Gather 'round, the tales begin,
Of love and loss, of what has been.
Every branch a voice, a friend,
In this haven, hearts will mend.

With laughter bright and eyes that shine,
We dive into stories, yours and mine.
Joyful moments shared with grace,
In this festive, enchanted place.

As stars emerge, our voices soar,
The echoes linger, wanting more.
In the boughs, our dreams take flight,
Filled with warmth, a pure delight.

Memories in the Grove

In the grove, laughter rings,
Where the sunlight softly clings.
Children dance beneath the trees,
Carried gently by the breeze.

Picnics spread on blankets wide,
Joy and warmth, a blissful tide.
Every bite and sip a cheer,
Filling hearts with love sincere.

Songs of old echo the past,
Moments cherished, stories cast.
Fireflies twinkle, night unfolds,
In the grove, a tale retold.

As stars above begin to gleam,
We weave together every dream.
Memories in love's embrace,
Forever held in nature's grace.

Gentle Giants Among Us

Beneath the boughs, giants stand tall,
Whispering secrets to one and all.
Branches spread like welcoming arms,
Nature's guardians, rich in charms.

In their shade, gatherings bloom,
Laughter brightens every room.
Stories shared like golden light,
Gentle giants guard the night.

Leaves shimmer in the soft breeze,
Dance and twirl with perfect ease.
As we celebrate life's great song,
With gentle giants, we belong.

Clouds drift by in a joyous array,
In the embrace of plants on display.
Together, we find our place,
In nature's arms, a warm embrace.

Nature's Evergreen Legacy

Among the pines, our spirits soar,
In the scent of pine, we explore.
Happiness sings in every tree,
Nature's gift, wild and free.

As seasons change, green leaves dance,
In their presence, we find a chance.
To celebrate the life we've known,
In every step, together grown.

Capricious winds bring laughter near,
As we gather, shedding all fear.
Hearts entwined with nature's thread,
A legacy in colors spread.

Together we cherish what remains,
In every heartbeat, love sustains.
An evergreen bond that will not fade,
In nature's arms, we are arrayed.

Serenade of the Green

In the park, a melody plays,
Nature's tune, a sweet ballet.
Petals flutter, colors sing,
A serenade of the green spring.

Children's laughter fills the air,
Sunshine gleams on their carefree hair.
Every blossom tells a tale,
Of joyous hearts that never pale.

With picnics laid upon the lawn,
We bask in light, until the dawn.
Moments cherished, shared, and bright,
In a world of joyful light.

As twilight whispers to the day,
Nature's magic won't decay.
A serenade that ever flows,
In the hearts where pure love grows.

Green Veil of Serenity

In whispers soft, the leaves will sway,
Beneath the sun's warm, golden ray.
A tapestry of vibrant green,
Where peace and joy are gently seen.

Morning dew on petals gleam,
Nature's beauty, like a dream.
Laughter dances on the breeze,
As hearts unite beneath the trees.

A gentle hum of life's sweet song,
In every valley, we belong.
With friends and families all around,
In this green haven, joy is found.

Raise a glass to moments shared,
To the love and peace that have been paired.
Together in this sacred space,
Where every smile brightens the place.

Nostalgia in Conifers

Underneath the conifers tall,
Memories rise, like a soft call.
With scents of pine in the air,
Old stories linger everywhere.

Childhood laughter, wild and free,
Echoes of what used to be.
Days of wonder, nights of stars,
Adventures waiting just beyond bars.

Fireflies dance in twilight's glow,
In the warmth of camaraderie, we know.
Every shade of green reflects,
The bonds we've built, the love connects.

As we gather 'round the flame,
Every heartbeat feels the same.
In the embrace of ancient trees,
Our spirits soar on gentle breeze.

Threads of Nature's Cloth

Woven colors, rich and bright,
Nature's canvas, pure delight.
From earth to sky, a vibrant thread,
In every garden, love is spread.

Petals whisper secrets sweet,
In unison, they rise and greet.
Beneath the warmth of sunny rays,
The world rejoices, sings, and plays.

Honey bees, they buzz around,
Crafting magic, nature's sound.
With every stitch, the world is sewn,
In unity, we have grown.

Gather 'round this joyful scene,
Life's rich fabric, lush and green.
Together we create and laugh,
In this tapestry, find our path.

Echoes of the Canopy

Beneath the arch of leaves above,
We celebrate the bonds of love.
Every rustle tells a tale,
As nature's whispers fill the vale.

With footsteps soft on forest floor,
Adventures wait behind each door.
The canopy, a shelter sweet,
Where harmony and laughter meet.

Sunlight breaks, a warm embrace,
We gather here in this sacred space.
Mountains high and rivers flow,
In nature's heart, our spirits grow.

Let voices rise in joyous cheer,
As friends and family gather near.
In echoes soft, our laughter flies,
Underneath these endless skies.

Reflections in the Woodlands

Beneath the boughs, a laughter rings,
The golden sun on water sings,
With every step, the leaves do sway,
A dance of joy, a bright bouquet.

Children play where shadows gleam,
A world alive as if a dream,
The whispers hold a tune so sweet,
Nature's rhythm guides our feet.

Flowers bloom in colors bold,
Stories of the forest told,
As twilight casts its gentle hue,
We weave our hopes, both old and new.

In every glance, the magic swirls,
In every heart, the joy unfurls,
With friends beside, we laugh and cheer,
In woodlands' realms, there's love, no fear.

Journey of the Sapling

From tiny seed to sprout so green,
Through whispered winds, a thriving dream,
With sunlit days and starlit nights,
The sapling grows, it feels the heights.

A gentle rain, a comforting kiss,
Each droplet sings a tune of bliss,
Roots dig deep in warm embrace,
A lifelong journey starts its race.

The seasons change, the colors shift,
Through storms' embrace, it learns to lift,
The sturdy trunk that holds its weight,
In every bend, it learns of fate.

With years it stands amidst the pines,
In every whisper, life aligns,
The journey long, yet oh so sweet,
In nature's heart, it finds its beat.

Breath of the Evergreen

In fragrant boughs, the breezes play,
The evergreen stands firm each day,
With needles bright, it greets the morn,
A timeless dance, forever born.

The winter's chill, it does embrace,
In snow-kissed silence, finds its place,
A cloak of white, so soft, divine,
The heart of nature, strong and fine.

In summer's sun, it sways so free,
A canvas painted brilliantly,
With every season, stories weave,
In whispered tales, we believe.

With every breath, the world exhales,
In harmony, where life prevails,
The evergreen, a steadfast friend,
In celebration, hearts will mend.

Timeworn Tales of the Trunks

Beneath the bark, a history glows,
With every ring, a secret flows,
The ages past, where whispers lie,
In starlit nights and azure sky.

Each gnarled twist holds tales untold,
Of summer's warmth, of winter's cold,
Through storms endured and sunlit days,
The trunks stand proud in nature's maze.

A child's laughter rings through leaves,
In every shadow, memory weaves,
The dance of branches, a timeless show,
In time's embrace, we learn and grow.

With playful winds, the stories catch,
In every heart, a new dispatch,
Timeworn trunks, both wise and keen,
In festive light, their tales are seen.

Mysterious Canopies

Underneath the leafy arch,
Colors dance in vibrant sways,
Laughter echoes through the trees,
Nature beckons, come and play.

Sunlight speckles through the green,
Whispers draw us near and far,
Every branch a secret keeps,
Winding paths beneath the star.

Joyful gatherings all around,
With friends we share the summer's song,
In this realm where dreams are spun,
A tapestry of life, so long.

Mysterious canopies invite,
Underneath their gentle sway,
Together we will laugh and twirl,
In the magic of the day.

Guardians of Time

Ancient trees with wisdom vast,
Standing tall, they watch and wait,
Branches cradle stories old,
Guardians of our fleeting fate.

In their shade, we gather close,
Hearts alight with tales to tell,
Every whisper in the breeze,
A connection, a gentle spell.

Seasons change, yet they remain,
Through storms and sunshine, they abide,
In their presence, we find peace,
A timeless bond, our spirits tied.

Underneath their watchful gaze,
We celebrate with joy and cheer,
In the embrace of nature's grace,
Guardians of time ever near.

Whispers of the Woodland

In the heart where shadows play,
Whispers drift on a soft breeze,
Nature calls with a gentle voice,
Calling us to pause with ease.

Mushrooms bloom in vibrant hues,
Ferns unfurl in silent grace,
Every step a dance anew,
Held in nature's warm embrace.

Fireflies twinkle like little stars,
Painting sparkles on the night,
Together, we ignite the dark,
A festival of heart delight.

The woodland sings, its secrets shared,
In this realm, our spirits soar,
In the whispers, we become one,
Nature's magic forevermore.

In the Company of Pines

Amidst the pines, we find our place,
Where laughter rings, and hearts align,
Under boughs in a green embrace,
Together we shall intertwine.

The scent of earth fills the air,
As whispers of the forest play,
Mirthful memories we will share,
In the company of friends today.

Above us, needles catch the sun,
Golden rays through branches fall,
In this haven, we have fun,
Nature's laughter, a joyful call.

With every step, a new delight,
Together we break free and roam,
In the company of pines so bright,
In this woodland, we are home.

Legacy of the Larch

Beneath the boughs, the laughter flies,
Children play beneath bright skies.
Golden leaves in the warm sunbeam,
Whispering tales, a joyful dream.

Gathering round with hearts so light,
Stories shared in the soft twilight.
Legacy flows in every cheer,
Echoes of love, forever near.

The larch stands tall, a guardian wise,
Celebrating moments, time never dies.
Together we sing, in harmony's nest,
A festival spirit, our hearts at rest.

With each step taken, the roots unite,
Dancing shadows in the fading light.
Our legacy shines in the embrace,
Of the larch's branches, a sacred space.

Stillness Among the Branches

In the stillness, a soft breeze sighs,
Rustling leaves, where the silence lies.
Nature's breath, a gentle charm,
Wrapped in peace, we come to harm.

Mellow moments invite us to stay,
While time dances, melting away.
Branches sway, with secrets and grace,
In this stillness, we find our place.

Colorful blooms surrounding the shade,
Each petal whispers, memories made.
Festive hearts in this quiet retreat,
The spirit is joyous, the atmosphere sweet.

We gather here in the warm embrace,
Of nature's bounty, a sacred space.
In this stillness, let laughter expand,
Together we weave, a festive strand.

In the Presence of the Tall

In the presence of giants, we gather round,
Their towering beauty, a wonder profound.
With each shared glance, we feel the mirth,
In their shadows, we celebrate our worth.

Twinkling lights in the canopy high,
As laughter rings out, reaching the sky.
Their sturdy arms cradle the songs we sing,
Joyous reminders of the hope they bring.

Among the tall, where dreams take flight,
The spirit of festivity ignites the night.
We dance through the twilight, hearts full and free,
In the presence of the tall, there's magic to see.

Every breath whispers of peace and delight,
A canvas of stars paints the deep night.
United we stand with the trees side by side,
In the presence of the tall, we share our pride.

Dance of the Fir

A dance begins in the soft moonlight,
Where echoes of laughter fill the night.
The fir takes the lead in a gentle sway,
Guiding our hearts, come join the play.

Ornaments glisten, a festive array,
As music of joy leads us away.
Each branch a partner, all stories unfold,
In the dance of the fir, we grow bold.

With every tree, our spirits entwine,
A tapestry woven, stories align.
As fireflies twinkle, we celebrate here,
In the dance of the fir, we conquer our fear.

Under the stars, with feet on the ground,
In the rhythm of nature, our hearts will surround.
Hand in hand, let the music inspire,
In the night's embrace, the dance of the fir.

Celestial Canopy

Stars twinkle above in delight,
As laughter spills into the night.
Glowing lanterns dance in the breeze,
Whispers of joy float through the trees.

Moonlight drapes a silver sheen,
On faces glowing, eyes agleam.
Together we share in this mirth,
Under the magic of the earth.

With music soaring, hearts take flight,
Each beat a pulse, pure and bright.
Celebration wraps us in its embrace,
A celestial night, a sacred space.

Let the world fade, just for now,
In this moment, we find a vow.
To dream, to dance, to live, to be,
Beneath the great canopy, wild and free.

Heartbeats Beneath the Leaves

In the forest, whispers hum,
Nature's rhythm, a steady drum.
Life pulsates in every shade,
As we gather, the world seems remade.

Colors burst with every sway,
Sunshine brightens the joyous play.
With every heartbeat, shadows weave,
A tapestry of dreams we believe.

Beneath the leaves, we spin and twirl,
In a dance that makes our hearts whirl.
Laughter mingles with birds in song,
In this moment, we all belong.

Embrace the warmth of every cheer,
With friends and family gathered near.
Together we bloom, never to part,
With heartbeats united, a festival of heart.

Resinous Memories

Beneath the boughs, laughter wove,
Golden sun in the stories we rove.
Resinous scents fill the air,
Whispers of joy, tender and rare.

With every glance, a tale unfolds,
Of adventures shared and secrets told.
Amidst the laughter, time stands still,
In this sacred space, we find our will.

Candles flicker with a gentle glow,
Casting shadows that ebb and flow.
Memories linger, sweet and strong,
In the heart of the night, we sing our song.

So raise a glass to moments past,
For the joy we share will ever last.
In resinous memories, we find release,
A festive spirit that brings us peace.

A Stillness Among the Sprouts

In spring's embrace, life begins anew,
A vibrant world bathed in morning dew.
Among the sprouts, a stillness lies,
As nature's canvas opens wide skies.

Colors blend in a delightful show,
As laughter rises, spirits glow.
Tiny blooms nod a gentle cheer,
A melody soft, yet crystal clear.

Gathered friends in joyous throng,
Finding harmony, where we belong.
Every heartbeat a whisper of cheer,
In this stillness, we hold each dear.

So let us dance where wild things sprout,
In the heart of nature, let joy shout.
Amidst the freshness of the day,
We celebrate life in our own way.

Unity of the Wildwood

In the heart of the forest, laughter rings,
Beneath the green arch where the robin sings.
Leaves shimmer bright in the golden light,
As nature's dance takes the edge of night.

With every step upon the mossy floor,
The world awakens, spirits soar.
A symphony plays, on the breeze it flows,
In wildwood's embrace, where friendship grows.

Gathered together, all hands entwined,
With joy and warmth, in our hearts aligned.
Under the stars, we share our delight,
In this unity, our souls ignite.

As the moonlight spills, painting the ground,
The wildwood whispers, a magic profound.
In every rustling leaf, a story we weave,
Unity of the wildwood, we believe.

Reverie in the Pines

Beneath tall pines, where shadows play,
A whispering breeze carries dreams away.
With laughter echoing through the trees,
In this reverie, we find our ease.

Sunlight dapples on the forest floor,
As we gather close, our spirits soar.
In the heart of the grove, we spin our tales,
Of joy and wonder as the laughter hails.

With pine-scented air, our worries fade,
In this festive heart, memories are made.
The world fades away, just us and the night,
In a reverie where everything feels right.

Stars watch over us, twinkling bright,
While the moonlight turns whispers into light.
Embracing the magic, side by side,
In the reverie of pines, we abide.

Legacy of the Evergreen

In a world aglow with emerald hues,
The evergreen stands, a tale to choose.
Branches stretched wide, like arms open wide,
In its shade, we gather, hearts swelling with pride.

With laughter like raindrops, we dance and sing,
Celebrating the joy that the moments bring.
Each whispering breeze carries stories we tell,
Of love, of laughter, where friendships dwell.

Through seasons of change, we hold our ground,
In the legacy of green, our joy is found.
With roots intertwined, we stand ever strong,
In the evergreen's embrace, we all belong.

As daylight fades to a star-studded sky,
We celebrate the bonds that will never die.
In the legacy of the evergreen's reign,
We find our solace, and we break every chain.

Chronicles of the Canopy

High above, where the sunlight gleams,
The canopy holds all our wildest dreams.
With branches entwined, a tapestry spun,
In the chronicles written, we all become one.

Birdsongs echo through layers of green,
In laughter and joy, solace is seen.
The canopy whispers, secrets unfold,
As our stories together are lovingly told.

On each leaf, a memory, bright as the day,
As we gather beneath in this festive display.
With hearts intertwined, and hands held tight,
In the chronicles of the canopy, we find our light.

As twilight descends, and stars fill the skies,
We share in the wonder, the laughter, the sighs.
In harmony stitched, like the stars that align,
Together we flourish, in this joy so divine.

www.ingramcontent.com/pod-product-compliance
Ingram Content Group UK Ltd.
Pitfield, Milton Keynes, MK11 3LW, UK
UKHW030845221224
452712UK00006B/505

9 789908 117898